11,530

;
.7
Do      Doering, Harald
          A bee is born.    Translated and adapted
        by Dale S. Cunningham.    N.Y., Sterling,
        [1973,c1962]
          96p.    illus.



          1.Bees.    I.Title.

STERLING NATURE SERIES

# A BEE
# IS BORN

### By Harald Doering

Translated and
adapted by
Dale S. Cunningham

## STERLING
Publishing Co., Inc.
New York

Oak Tree Press Co., Ltd. London & Sydney

Eighth Printing, 1973

Copyright © 1973, 1962
by Sterling Publishing Co., Inc.
419 Park Avenue South, New York, N.Y. 10016
British edition published by Oak Tree Press Co., Ltd., Nassau, Bahamas
Distributed in Australia and New Zealand by Oak Tree Press Co., Ltd.,
P.O. Box 34, Brickfield Hill, Sydney 2000, N.S.W.
Distributed in the United Kingdom and elsewhere in the British Commonwealth
by Ward Lock Ltd., 116 Baker Street, London W 1
*Manufactured in the United States of America*          *All rights reserved*
Library of Congress Catalog Card No.: 62-18626
ISBN 0–8069-3502–2          UK 7061– 2253–4
3503–0

# TABLE OF CONTENTS

Honeybee
engraved on a
Greek tetradrachma
from 387-295 B.C.

# Index

# A BEE IS BORN

Busy, noisy, ceaselessly buzzing and working, the honeybee's life revolves around the geometrically-perfect cells of its homemade comb of wax. There it raises its brood and stores its honey. The queen of the colony is a fertile female. She is the focal point of each bee family with its thousands of worker bees—infertile females who do all the work. They gather and prepare the food, produce the wax and perform all of the varied services needed in a small city. Some worker bees are cleaning ladies; many serve as nursemaids, tending the babies and young bees, feeding them and keeping them warm; others are construction workers, water carriers, guards, pall-bearers and even specialists in preserving food.

Actually, not all bees are busy bees. In the bee society the stingless males—the drones—do no work!

For thousands of years honeybees and their wonderfully organized society have fascinated mankind. In fact, bees are older than man; in a piece of amber 43 million years old, a honeybee can be seen preserved, with its pollen basket still intact!

Scientists have studied the regimented life of the bee over the centuries. Even with all that is known about bees, their activities are so interesting and so remarkable that we never tire of investigating further. Without bees, many flowers and plants would be without seed, for the bee carries the pollen from blossom to blossom to fertilize them. The bee is generally faithful to one type of blossom. Though plants are dependent on the bees for pollination, the bees, in turn, must have the plant's

This bee is 43 million years old! Imprisoned in a piece of amber known to be of that age, the bee looks exactly like a modern bee.

nectar to convert into honey, and the plant's pollen as a source of protein and vitamins.

What creature but a bee communicates with others of its kind in so well-developed a language? The bee can say, for example, with the help of its dance-language, "We have just discovered an apple orchard in full bloom. It is about 350 yards from here toward the sun. There we found nectar free for the taking."

Bees and their colonies are like men and their cities in more ways than one. On certain occasions, bees vote in what seems like a genuinely democratic manner—the majority may decide where to live if a choice is available.

# LITTLE CITIZENS IN A LARGE COMMUNITY

FROM ITS earliest beginnings until the very end of its existence, for better or worse, the honeybee's life is linked with its community as closely as a leaf's with a tree. Alone, it would quickly die, for the honeybee is a *social* creature which needs its colony in order to exist.

For the survival of the colony, nature arranges for each member bee to perform specific chores. These functions change according to the age of the honeybee and the immediate needs of the colony. In each colony are many thousands of workers—females whose reproductive organs are not developed; one queen—the only fertile female; and a few hundred drones—whose only duty is to try to be the queen's husband. If the colony is in a good location, and if the weather is normal and other outside conditions upon which bees depend are normal, a colony can grow to a population of 60,000.

All bees, including the hornet, wasp, and bumblebee, live this way. But the honeybee is destined for an even more arduous life than other social bees, for nature decided further that the honeybee, like the ant, must provide for the future. Its colony is perennial, carrying on its family life even during cold, barren winters. The other bee and insect colonies are annual, with all but the queen dying out in the fall. From the first buddings of the plants and trees, all through the spring and summer, the worker honeybees continuously fly about, gathering

(Left) These workers are on the brood cells, tending the larvae. In the upper part of the comb can be seen a few storage cells packed with pollen.

nectar and pollen not only for immediate nourishment, but also to store up in the cells of the hive. This food will tide the colony over periods of rain and seasons when no plants are in bloom.

Because of this endless work during flower-blooming time, a worker honeybee hatched in spring or early summer is soon worn out and dies after about 40 days. Workers hatched late in summer or in the autumn have less active lives and can look forward to a life span of about 8 months, living through the winter in a semi-conscious state and carrying on the work of the hive in the early spring. Drones live from late spring to the end of summer. Only the queen will live longer than one year; she can live for as long as 5 years, but many calamities can befall her, too, and alter the course of her life, as we shall see later.

By the end of winter the queen begins to lay eggs so

Close-up view of the brood cells showing larvae in various stages of development, but all prior to the closing of the lid. In the top row can be seen a newly laid egg.

Here in a wax cell is the thin, worm-like egg of a worker laid by the queen barely 3 hours ago. Before this, the cell was cleaned and polished by the worker bees. The queen had to satisfy herself that the cell was clean before lowering her body into it. She lays the egg exactly in the middle of the bottom, attaching it horizontally to the bottom wall. The cell, which has a slight upward slope, has been cut open lengthwise and enlarged 10 times.

that she will have enough adult honey-gatherers ready to work by spring. Most important to the colony are the first early-blooming plants, such as the pussy willow and the maple tree, the snowdrop and the crocus. They provide the protein-rich pollen necessary for rearing the brood.

The eggs are laid in a part of the hive called the brood chamber. One square inch of the brood chamber contains about 28 small cells for eggs which are destined to be workers, or 18 larger cells for drones; cells designed to rear a queen are the largest of all.

# THE WORKER – FROM EGG TO BEE

THE LIFELINE of each colony is the worker—the busiest of all bees. Hatched from a queen's fertilized egg, it enters a life of toil and service from the moment it hatches. To ensure the survival of her family, the queen lays many thousands of worker eggs each season.

Like drones and the queen, workers have 4 wings, 6 hairy legs with hooked feet, sense organs, a sucking tongue and biting jaws. But only the workers have, in addition, organs for making wax and special apparatus for collecting nectar and pollen.

(Left) In the upper left of the top picture we see the egg from above. The egg hatches a tiny larva (open cell at the right) in 72 hours. This larva is fed a special food, royal jelly, by nursing bees for the first 60 hours, followed by about 84 hours of pollen and honey feeding. The rate of growth is enormous. A larva gains 1500 times its original weight within 144 hours. A human baby with the same rate of growth would be the size of a hippopotamus after a few days! During this feeding and growth period the larva moults (sheds its skin) four times in all, once a day at the beginning of its development.

The larvae shown in the semiclosed cells are about 120 hours old and are in the pollen and honey feeding stage. The cell entrances are still open so the nursing bees can feed the larvae (for another 24 hours), after which they will be closed with a wax lid and the larvae will enter the next stage of development.

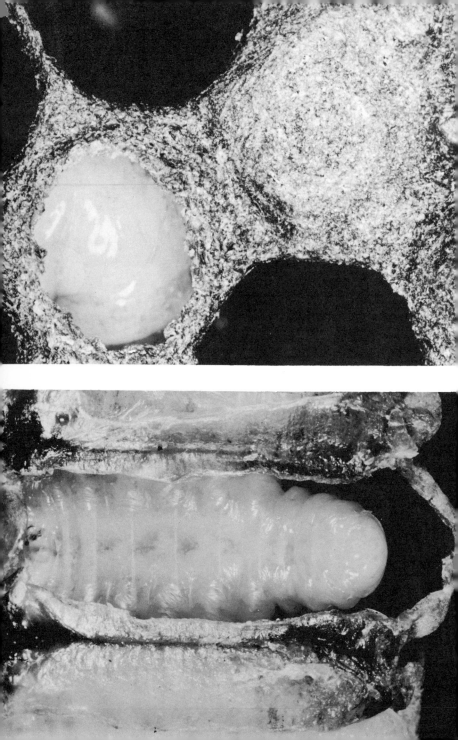

(Left) To make a cover for the cell, the adult bees knead out the thickened wax of the cell edge somewhat as a baker kneads and spreads his dough. In the cell to the left the bees have only begun to knead the wax. They continue to spread it until the cell is covered as completely as the one to the right. This wax cover allows just enough air to pass through to ventilate the growing larva. In the security of the covered cell, the larva stretches itself out and spins its cocoon.

(Left) This cell, cut open lengthwise, shows a 10-day-old larva stretched out into a long, narrow shape and enveloped in its cocoon.

(Left) The cocoon stage lasts only 2 or 3 days and then the larva sheds its cocoon. Soon after this last moulting, it becomes a pupa. In this stage, it starts out all white. Then a change begins, the eyes turn first pink, then purple, and finally black-brown. Coloration starts with the eyes and steadily works back to the rear.

(Below) This pupa (16 days old counting from egg-laying) is in the stage when the final forms of the body, wings and legs are developed.

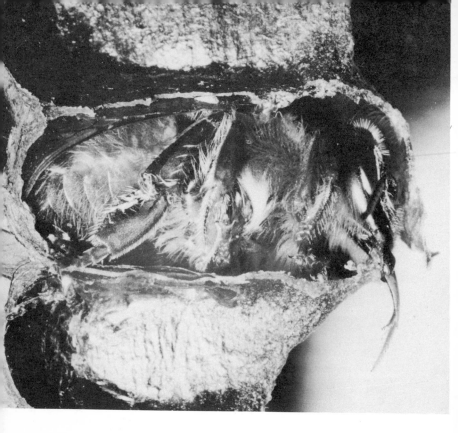

(Above) The sleep in the pupa stage lasts 9 days. Then begins
the birth process which will free it from its covered cell.

(Right) The hatching insect has nibbled out a small opening in
the wax cover and is hungrily sticking out its tongue.

**18**

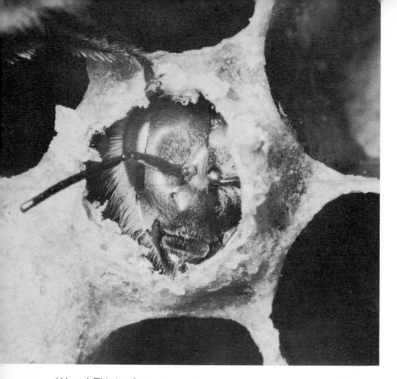

(Above) This is a front view of the same hatching insect (about 18 times enlarged). The work of nibbling through the wax cover has exhausted it, and it sticks out its tongue to get food from passing nurse bees. Refreshed by the feeding, the bee starts to work again. It gnaws at the previously protective wax cover, which is now only in the way. Soon it will climb from its cell.

(Below) Later the bee's tongue, or *glossa*, which is shaped like a bottle-washing brush, will be used to harvest nectar from the flowers in the field.

With the effective help of the older bees, the wax
cover has now been completely gnawed away, and the
young bee can hatch. A short life full of adventures,
endless work and danger awaits her.

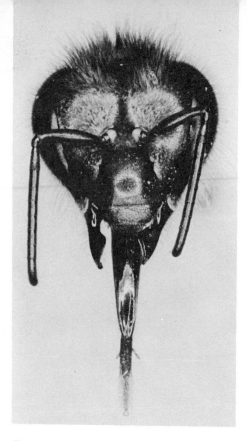

Close-up view of the bee's head
with the *glossa* (tongue) extended.

(Right, opposite page) About 21 days after the egg is laid, this newly born worker emerges. Standing unsteadily on its 6 legs, it has silvery, glistening wings and a fluffy, soft coat, unscarred and untorn. In time, this delicate creature will become a black old veteran, bruised and worn out by constant activity and battles with the elements and its enemies.

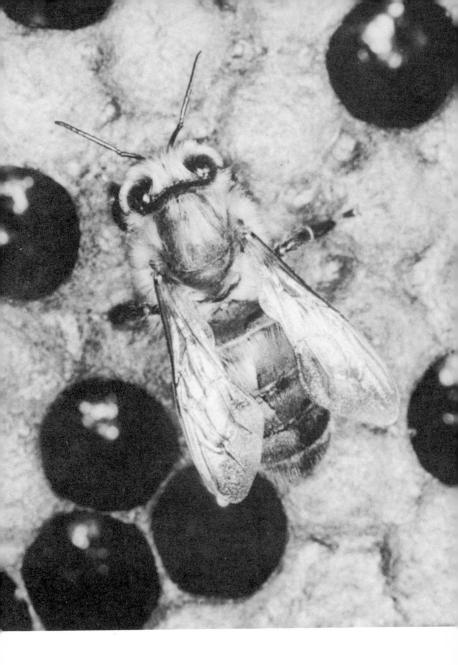

(Left) These two young bees are cleaning empty cells.

(Below) Worker dragging dead bee out of hive.

# THE BUSY LIFE OF THE WORKER BEE

FROM THE moment the female worker bee is hatched, she has her tasks clearly cut out for her. Since she does not yet possess fully developed glands for nursing the larvae in the brood, she makes herself useful at other household chores inside the hive.

## House-cleaning Ladies

The first task of the young workers is to clean out the cells. All the remains left behind by the hatching insects must be removed from the brood cells before the queen will lay more eggs in them; she will avoid any cell which is not immaculate. The wax cells that will hold honey also must be thoroughly cleansed and smoothed out before the precious honey that will nourish the colony through the winter can be stored in them without danger of contamination.

## The Clean-up Squads

Preventing disease is an important function in the bee world. To keep infection from spreading from the decaying bodies of bees that have died in the hive, the workers carry the corpses outside and cast them as far away as possible from the entrance. Usually, however, bees will die outside the hive where they cannot harm the colony.

Enemy insects which have crawled into the hive, bees from other colonies which have forced their way in, and other intruders bent on stealing the honey, are stung to death by the hive's guardians; these, too, are carried out by the undertakers.

Larger honey thieves, such as mice, that have paid with their lives for their presumption, but are too large to be carried out of the hive, are treated in a unique manner. The workers seal them in bee glue (*propolis*), a substance the bees make from a brown resin they collect from trees. In the hot, dry air of the hive, these sealed corpses become mummified and in this preserved state they are no longer a source of infection.

## Nursing Duty

During the first 5 days, while the workers are serving as house-cleaners, their nursing glands mature. Then for the next 7 days they are able to feed the young

(Above) The nurses cover up the cells, too. Here, two nurses are kneading out the thick wax at the edge of a cell, to form a cover through which air can pass.

larvae on "bee milk" or royal jelly, which is secreted by their nursing glands. The food given differs according to its age and what it will become—worker, drone or queen. The queen, of course, is fed royal jelly throughout her life.

(Left, opposite page) A nurse is busy visiting a larva. This happens several thousand times for every larva—a tremendous amount of work for the busy bees. The larva, however, is not fed on every visit.

# THE QUEEN – HEART OF THE COLONY

IN EACH colony of bees there is one monarch—the queen. Largest and longest of all the bees, she is the only honeybee without which the colony cannot survive. From larva to adult insect, her existence is different in every way from that of the worker or the drone. The cell in which she is reared is larger than those of the workers and drones, is irregular in shape and, unlike the horizontal worker and drone cells, hangs vertically.

Because of the royal destiny of the eggs laid in these cells, the nurse bees serve them a steady diet of royal jelly throughout the larval stage. Royal jelly, or "bee milk," is a special food which the worker bees produce in their nursing glands. All larvae are fed royal jelly at first, but the workers are switched to a mixture of pollen and honey after the first 60 hours. Possibly this difference in diet accounts for the fact that the queen lives so long and that the female worker bees do not develop complete reproductive organs.

The queen has longer legs than a worker and also a large abdomen. In the latter are two ovaries where her eggs develop. She may lay half a million eggs altogether.

(Left) The queen in the hive can always be found by looking for an area where the worker bees are facing each other. In the middle of this court will be the queen.

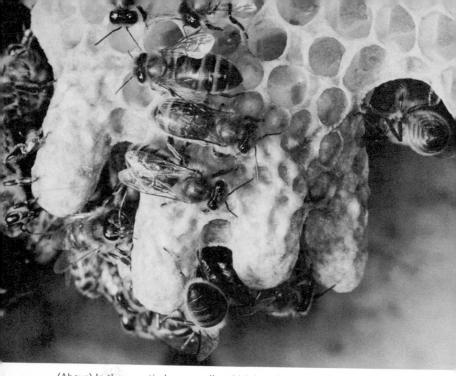

(Above) In these vertical queen cells, which have just been closed by the workers, lie queen larvae. Several queen cells are built by the workers to be sure that at least one will survive the early stages of development. The first to hatch will become the reigning queen. The remainder will be killed.

A great majority of the eggs are fertilized by male sperm which the queen receives from one or more drones on her mating flights, and which she stores for use all through her life. These fertilized eggs develop into workers (or queens). In the summer she also lays some unfertilized eggs which develop into drones.

(Right) This is the way the larva of a queen bee lies in a queen cell which has just been closed. Above the larva is some royal jelly.

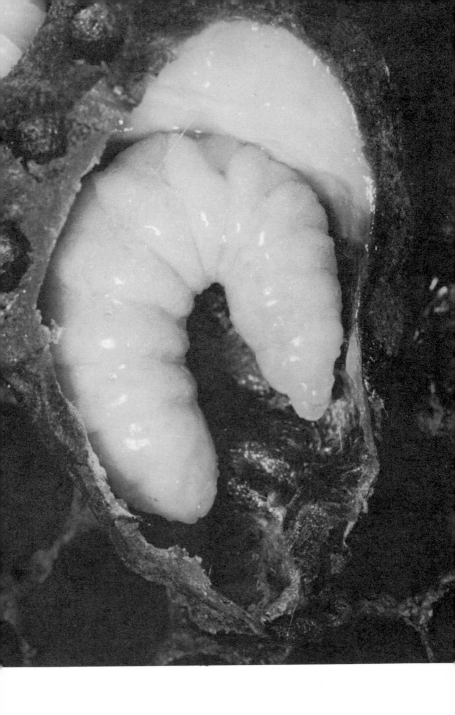

The future queen has already pupated and her coloration has begun to change at the eyes. The new ruler will soon hatch. While the development of a worker takes about 21 days from egg to adult bee, a queen hatches 5 days earlier.

In this sequence (above and the two following pages) the queen starts to nibble open the lid of her cell; then she is almost free; and, finally, she climbs out of her cell.

On all but a few occasions the queen's life is confined to her brood nest in the interior of the hive. A few days after climbing from her hatching cell, she may go on a short orientation flight which prepares her for her mating flight or flights later. On the mating flights, she is pursued by the male bees (drones). One or more of these drones catch her and deposit sperm in her abdomen. She can then begin her reign of egg-laying.

Almost free

The queen is hatched

The first of the young queens to escape from her cell will not tolerate the presence of other young queens. Her first act often consists of stinging to death any competing queens. This can lead to a vicious battle between rivals of equal strength, each trying to kill the other by stinging her. The queen's lancet has only partly developed barbs so that she does not lose it—and her life—when defending herself.

The other occasion on which the queen leaves the hive is at swarming time. About half the bees in the colony then go with her to found a new colony. They leave in the hive several capped queen cells, one of which will hatch into a queen for the "parent" colony from which the swarm came.

Having killed one rival almost her own age, the queen has bitten open the protective covering of cells containing unhatched queens and is stinging them to death.

Note the queen's long tapering abdomen, ideal for egg-laying.

The queen starts laying each year in early spring and lays more and more eggs each day until she reaches 2,000 eggs a day in early summer. She then gradually slows down until winter sets in. The worker bees feed her on royal jelly, which enables her to lay so many eggs. After about 2 or 3 seasons, a queen's ability to lay eggs usually diminishes, but she may live 4 or 5 years.

The queen is the key to the continuance of the colony. One of the glands in her head secretes the "queen substance," and this becomes distributed over her entire body. Since she is constantly licked and preened by the nurse bees, the substance is absorbed by these workers who, in turn, distribute it throughout the family in the food they pass on. As long as there is sufficient queen substance to satisfy the colony, it remains a single unit, no swarming takes place and no new queen is raised to supersede the present queen.

If a queen dies or is lost (perhaps killed by a careless beekeeper) the bees are aware of their loss within half an hour for the continuous transmission of the queen substance ceases. Agitated, they search everywhere for their queen. Enthusiasm for work flags, as if the bees knew that a queenless colony may be condemned to death.

There is, however, one possible salvation for a queenless colony. Cinderella's godmother performed no greater miracle than this: if the lost queen has left some of her fertilized eggs or very young larvae not more than a few days old, the workers can raise a new queen! They do this by enlarging the ordinary-sized workers' cell to the size of a queen cell, and meanwhile feed the larva living in the cell on a copious supply of royal jelly. And, lo and behold, from the egg of a dead ruler emerges a new queen!

Now if the new queen makes her mating flight safely, the colony is safe. Many dangers confront all young queens outside the hive. It has recently been discovered that the workers "exercise" a young queen by chasing her about inside the hive. In this way her muscles develop and she is able to fly confidently and swiftly.

With all the skills of architect and engineer combined, these workers are laying the "foundation" for their new comb. Suspended in a still, straight row, they are forming little wax plates in their abdomens.

## BRICKLAYERS AND CONSTRUCTION WORKERS

From the 13th to the 16th days of their lives, worker bees devote themselves chiefly to the building trade. In addition, when necessary, they shift to water-carrying. In fact, whenever an emergency disturbs the normal routine of the hive, the workers will pitch in wherever they are needed. Even bees belonging to different age groups will leave their regular assignments to help in the afflicted area. How they know what service they must perform at each stage and during each crisis, is still something we do not fully understand.

Bees in the construction forces secrete little wax "bricks" of dull-yellow "beeswax." Their wax-producing glands lie on the underside of the abdomen.

Actually, these bricks are merely tiny flakes of wax—so tiny that it takes almost half a million flakes to make only a pound of wax!

During the wax-making process the workers appear to be asleep as they cling quietly to each other, lined up like soldiers in a "building chain." After a bee expels a flake, bristles on its hind legs spear it and bring it up to the chewing organs (mandibles). With the hairline accuracy of engineers, the honeybees systematically process the wax into walls for hexagonal (six-sided) cells in the comb. These walls are from 1/280 to a sheer 1/500 of an inch thin! Extra wax must be used to rein-

Here in detail is a section of the underside of a bee's abdomen magnified about 30 times.

force the upper edges (the cells are built from the top down) so that they will not be crushed by the weight of the workers running across them in the course of their daily activities. But the economical bees do not waste even this small amount of extra wax—later they will knead it to make covers for honey and brood cells.

The solid beeswax becomes pliable when warm and if the combs get overheated they can melt and fall down, causing great destruction in the colony.

The construction of a new comb requires exceptional ingenuity and foresight. Since bees always start building from the top, the roof must be sturdy enough to support the hanging weight of the rest of the dwelling, the new brood, and later when the combs are laden with honey, several additional pounds of weight.

A honeycomb is truly one of nature's wonders. Marvellously efficient and economical, it is built entirely from the wax produced in the bee's body; cracks and unused small spaces are "cemented" with bee glue (*propolis*). Its walls are delicately thin, yet strong enough to hold several pounds of honey. The hexagonal cells are built side by side, each midrib serving for two cells; their sizes are designed to fit the sizes of the kind of bees which will hatch from them. To prevent the honey and larvae from spilling out, the cells slope slightly from the horizontal down toward the middle of the comb.

With the "building chain" of workers acting as a carpenter's plumb-line, the comb always hangs in a straight, vertical line. When the first comb is well on the way to completion, other combs are started on each side of it, then additional combs are added until all the available space is used. Wild bees usually settle in the hollows of trees, in caves, or sometimes in holes in walls or roofs.

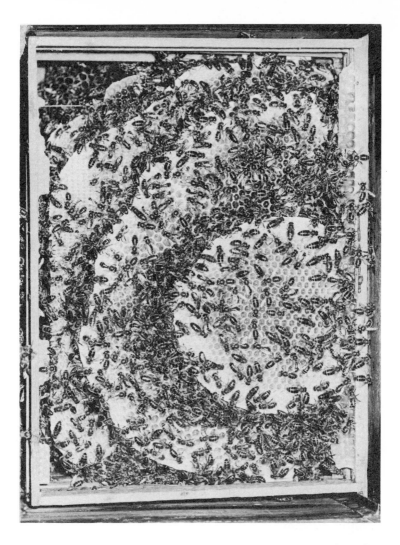

In a single night, these wizards of the insect world have completed this comb, a structure of amazing architectural beauty combined with functional design. With cells on both sides, a comb of this size contains about 6,000 cells. No electronic brain could devise a storage dwelling with greater efficiency, with less expenditure of material, or in so short a time. Yet bees built this marvel without a single instrument. In this short while, too, nectar has been stored in the finished cells; these can be distinguished by the reflections of light from the bottoms of the cells.

Sitting peacefully next to each other these water carriers avidly pump themselves full of water.

# THE BEE'S BUILT-IN THERMOSTAT

As THE seasons change from hot to cool to freezing, the bees use various methods to maintain a completely steady temperature of 95 degrees inside and around the brood nest. For this purpose bees are endowed with an organism of such great sensitivity that it enables them to gauge perfectly any variation in temperature to within a mere half-degree Fahrenheit.

## Cooling System

On a hot summer day when the temperature soars to heights that would overheat the wax cells if left unremedied, a corps of construction workers take over as emergency water carriers.

They pump themselves full of water, carry it back to

An enlargement of the tongue being used for sucking up the water.

When the temperature rises inside the hive, bees can be seen fanning to change the air and ventilate the hive. When bees fan at the entrance to the hive with their scent glands open, they are "scenting." (See page 73.)

the dwelling threatened by heat, and spray it lightly over the brood comb. Rapidly, the bees beat their wings and fan the moistened cells, causing heat to be drawn off through evaporation. This prevents the brood nest temperature from going above 95 degrees Fahrenheit. A two-fold catastrophe is avoided—the destruction of the home and the death of the helpless brood.

## Heating System

When the hot summer fades and chilly autumn comes on, the workers use different methods to safeguard their family against the cold. To protect the brood they huddle over the brood comb, forming a blanket as warm as a fine layer of down feathers. (See photo on right.) To produce additional heat, they burn the sugar in their little bodies by vibrating their wings. (If you look closely at a bee trying to produce heat, you actually can see its wings vibrating slightly.) When the winter's frost grips the land, the bees protect themselves from freezing by balling closely together into the "winter cluster."

A bee uses up most fuel when it is flying, but even then it is an extremely small amount; 3,000 bees can

Guards stand
in military rows
at the
flight entrance.

fly for an hour on a single ounce of sugar. While flying, a bee beats its wings up and down about 200 times a second. It is estimated that with this rapid wing beat, it flies at a rate of about 12 miles an hour. No man-made engine can fly this fast with so little fuel!

## GUARD DUTY

EACH BEE family must protect its store of honey, for many creatures covet this treasure. Even bees from different colonies in the same apiary send out spies and scouts to locate large honey supplies and direct invading forces of looters to them. Guard duty falls to workers from about the 16th to the 20th days of their lives. Like army sentinels, they watch over the gates of their golden city of honey—sometimes flying around the landing-board entrance, sometimes standing in front of it in strict rank and file, always ready for immediate take-off.

Every arriving bee is inspected to see if it is a *bona fide*

On guard duty.

Arriving bee is inspected by the guard. Its arched back reveals it is an enemy.

The invader expels large doses of its scent, hoping to befuddle the guard.

Auxiliary troops rush to the scene, and the enemy is overwhelmed.

At last, the guard is able to get a tight grip on the enemy, lift it up, and throw it over the landing board.

citizen of the colony. Strangers are detected by differences in scent, and also by tell-tale movements, such as the arched back of an attacker. Drones, being harmless, may come and go, but all other foreign bees are stung to death or mercilessly driven away. If necessary,

Now a wasp,
bent on stealing
honey, tries to slip
by the guard while
its back is turned.

In the murderous
battle that develops,
they turn over and
under, each trying
to manoeuvre into
stinging position.

Locked together in
a life-or-death
struggle, they
repeatedly plunge
their stingers into
each other's bodies.

The contestants
are evenly matched.
At this point the
outcome of the
battle is
undecided.

As though a call to
arms has been
sounded, reserve
guards rush to the
scene.

Finally the wasp is
stung to death,
and the reserve
troops prepare to
toss it off the
landing board.

The attacking guard is coming straight for the camera! It heads for the author-photographer as if drawn by an invisible magnet, undaunted even by so large a foe.

additional workers are drafted, and the battle develops into a life-or-death struggle.

Not only are foreign bees, wasps, hornets, mice, and bears attacked, but also the greatest honey thief of all—man!

After a few moments of furious aerial combat almost any enemy worker is completely repelled. The guards immediately resume their posts for the next encounter.

After stinging a man, a bee must die. Instinct alone compels the bee to fulfill this fatal duty, not a conscious willingness to sacrifice its life. Since it can withdraw its lancet without danger from insects, it is not forewarned against man. It cannot know that its poison spear and venom sac will be ripped from its body when the lancet remains embedded in the soft flesh of a warm-blooded animal.

Reaching its target, the bee plunges its
stinger into the photographer's finger,
penetrating the skin.

# WEAPONS: STINGERS AND VENOM

THE WORKER BEE'S stinging mechanism is a tiny precision instrument made up of no fewer than 20 different parts. Venom from a poison sac is forced through a narrow channel between two tough lancets held rigid by a hard sheath, and into the intended victim through 20 or more recurved barbs (teeth slanted away from the direction of entry). After the sting, when the bee pulls away, the barbs force the lancets to remain (like fish hooks) in the warm-blooded victim's flesh. The stinger continues to bore deeper, by reflex movements, and release poison in the wound, so it is wise to extract the stinger immediately (without squeezing if possible) if you get stung. The bee cannot live long without its stinger and poison sac.

Very young bees cannot sting, as a full supply of venom is not produced until the bees reach an age when they undertake guard duties.

Some people are allergic to bee venom and become seriously (even fatally) ill from a single sting. However, bee stings more often cause a moment of sharp pain followed by fear of the poison's effect, which can be worse than the minor discomfort of the swelling. A researcher I used to know once proved that even injecting the venom of 2,000 bees directly into the bloodstream of a horse had no other effect than to produce a slight fever. On the other hand, bee venom has been used as a remedy for some ailments, such as rheumatism.

This bee is flying away, leaving its stinger and poison sac behind, held by recurved barbs, in the soft warm flesh of the finger.

This bee stands on the edge of the landing board poised for its first take-off for outside service. From a life chiefly confined to the darkness inside the hive, it now flies out into a world of sun and flowers.

## OUTDOOR WORK

ABOUT THE twentieth day of its life the worker graduates from inside duties, and ventures outdoors. For the rest of its short life it will be a field worker, gathering nectar and pollen.

Before the first official supply-gathering expeditions, the bee makes short test flights which beekeepers call orientation or "play" flights. It flies around the vicinity of the hive and hovers about the entrance, flying backwards at times, imprinting on its memory the surroundings of the hive and exact location of the entrance.

The pungent smell attracts this fast-moving bee.

Daily during the summer months, thousands of worker bees fly out of their hives for the first time. In good weather you can see them testing their aeronautic skills in front of their hives, a fascinating exhibit that seldom lasts more than half an hour at a time.

Now begins the heavy work of gathering supplies. The gatherers must make numerous flights, sometimes ranging a mile or more, in search of pollen and nectar. To gather pollen, a bee rummages about in the flowers until its body is completely dusted with the pollen. With the bristle-like hairs on its forelegs, it then combs the pollen off and packs it into pollen baskets on its two hind legs, using a tiny bit of nectar to make it stick more securely. Not wasting a second of its precious time,

**59**

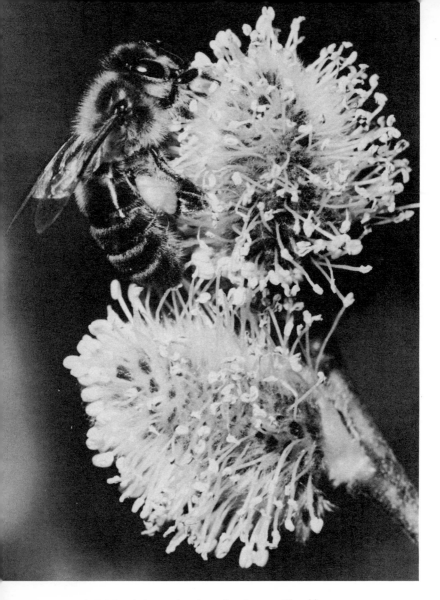

(Above) This bee is harvesting the pollen from a willow blossom.

(Right) Each hive of bees is faithful to one type of plant. This bee is about to get pollen from a nasturtium.

**60**

This bee is dusting itself with apple-blossom pollen. Its honey will taste of apple.

62

A bee returning to the hive with its pantaloon-like pollen baskets well filled.

it continues fastening the pollen in mid-air while flying from one flower to another!

The food value of pollen for the honeybee varies with different types of plants. Among the most valuable are willow blossoms, which yield the proteins and vitamins most essential to the diet of the young brood and even of adult bees, especially in the spring when the bee's year begins. Some cone-bearing (coniferous) trees produce pollen which is almost without value to the bees. Unfortunately, the bees, which are so efficient in other ways, cannot judge the differences in the food value of various types of pollen. (In fact, bees have even been seen gathering coal dust.)

Bees in this modern world can gather another substance besides pollen and nectar. In the last few years, scientists have transported bee colonies to danger zones of nuclear test areas to help determine the amount of radioactive fall-out. They let the bees loose. When they return to the hive, Geiger counters measure the amount of strontium in the nectar and pollen.

Even when the fields are checkered with blossoms of many kinds of plants, each individual bee remains faithful to one kind of plant. This is nature's way of using the honeybee to fertilize, or pollinate, the fields and orchards. The honeybee carries the pollen, or male product, to the stigma, or female part, of the same kind of blossom. This is important because the pollen from one species of flower will not fertilize another species.

Without this direct pollination by the bees, much pollen would be lost in the wind or left to die in the flower cup, and many plants would not bloom another season. So important is this pollinating that the yield of fruit orchards and fields in which bees have settled is much greater than those in which no bee colony

The worker hovering
over the landing board
is returning
with a full supply
of nectar.

dwells. This service of the bees adds to the market millions of pounds of fruits and flowers!

To plants dependent on bee pollination, nature has given beautiful flamboyance and strong sweet scents to attract bees. Where brightness and pungent scents

The nectar is spread out to evaporate by being carried around from cell to cell on the bees' tongues. It becomes more and more condensed, until finally, after a long time and a great deal of work, it is ready to become honey. Then, it is carefully stored away in a supply cell.

are lacking, the bees are apparently attracted to pollen-rich blooms by the vibrations set up in even the slightest breeze. Markings on the flowers, called "nectar guides," acting as signposts, run down into the flower cup (calyx) from the outside and lead the bees to stores of nectar. Safety guards growing in the bottom of the calyx keep the bees from slipping off while they suck the sweet fluid and dust themselves with pollen.

Some plants, such as sage, have intricate mechanisms which are operated automatically by the weight of the bees. A bee landing on one of these plants, presses down a lever and triggers a mechanism that deposits a packet of pollen on the bee's body to be carried to the next plant.

In nature's sensible order of creation, both the flowers and the bees flourish in a mutually profitable association. The pollen that the bees harvest for their own use is carried back to the hive. To keep it from decaying, it is treated with fluids secreted from the bees' bodies, then deposited in storage cells. Pollen cells are filled to about $\frac{3}{4}$ capacity and are not capped or sealed as are honey cells.

Just as a bee is equipped with rear legs designed especially for carrying pollen, it has an extra "social" stomach designed especially for transporting nectar and honey. Lying in front of a smaller stomach that nourishes the bee itself, this honey stomach or nectarsac receives nectar intended for the whole colony.

Honeybees condense nectar into honey by drying it out in the hive, but the process from nectar to honey is a long one. It takes 3 ounces of nectar to produce *one* ounce of honey. In order to harvest a teaspoonful of honey for our breakfast a bee would have to fly a total of about 1,250 miles and make millions of landings.

"Cook" laying in the honey.

About 200,000 trips between flowers and hive are required to make an ounce of honey; for one pound a single bee would have to circle the earth about three times.

The nectar is not only condensed by being stretched in a thin film on the bees' tongues and being exposed to the air that way, but also an important enzyme (invertase) is added which breaks down the predominantly sucrose sugar (table sugar) in nectar into two simple sugars (levulose and dextrose). When a cell is full of honey, workers close it with a wax cover just as a housewife seals a jar of preserves. Unlike the cover of a brood cell, which lets air through, the cover of a honey cell is airtight.

Honey is of course the reason why man keeps bees. From earliest Biblical times until well into the Middle Ages, honey was the only substance people had available to sweeten their foods. Later, honey was largely replaced by the introduction of cane sugar.

A beekeeper can collect 100 pounds of honey from a single colony in a good year. Of course he is not so foolish as to leave the bees without any supplies, for the colony still needs quite a bit of food for winter consumption. As a substitute for the honey, modern beekeepers feed their bees sugar, to assure them of sufficient winter stores.

(Below) Bees do not scorn a tasty morsel. If they can refresh themselves at a drop of finished honey, they make use of this opportunity without hesitation.

Two bees feed each other. This mutual sharing of food goes on continually every-where in the hive.

# FOOD SHARING

INTERCHANGE of food goes on all the time in the hive, and it serves several purposes. The foragers (gatherers) are quickly relieved of their nectar loads and can go off for another load. The house bees, whose glands are developed for feeding the brood, receive nourishment without spending time in fetching food. The passing of food back and forth helps to ripen the nectar into honey by adding various enzymes to it. Finally, with the food, the queen substance is also distributed throughout the colony, and this welds it into one whole queen-right community.

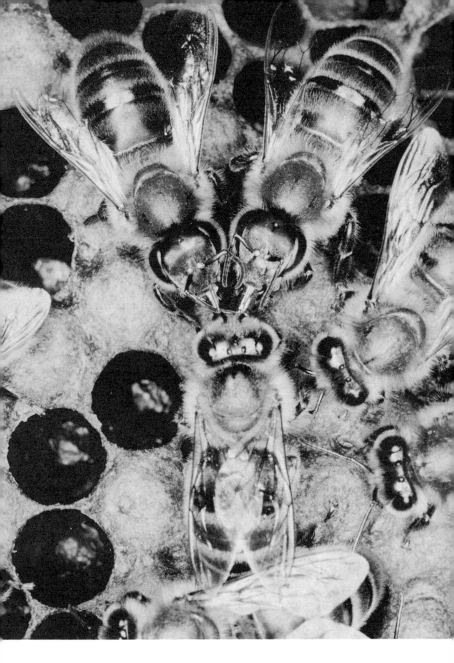

Returning gatherers feed some of the nectar they have harvested to the inside workers.

This bee, practically standing on its
head, is vigorously "scenting."

# SCENTING AND FANNING

THE CERTAINTY with which each bee finds its way back to the flight hole of its own hive is truly amazing. Their secret "radar" is provided by the "scenting" bees on the landing board in times of emergency.

Standing alone or in groups in front of the entrance to their colony, scenting bees hold their abdomens high and move their wings almost incessantly to fan the scent. If you look closely between the last and the next to the last segment of the abdomen you will notice the slightly extended scent gland. A scent characteristic to the particular colony escapes from this gland, and the bee disperses it around the hive opening by beating its wings.

Bees do this "scenting" whenever it is necessary to broadcast the location of the colony to all its members, as for instance after a swarm has been put into a new hive.

Bees also air-condition their hive.

Different beating of wings inside the hive, without exposing the scent gland, is called "fanning." Bees fan to change the air and ventilate the hive. Fanning keeps the brood-nest temperature from going above 95 degrees Fahrenheit. If the humidity is too low, fanning raises it by speeding the evaporation of the water brought in by the water carriers. If the humidity is too high, fanning moves the air and thereby reduces it. Finally, fanning helps condense nectar into honey.

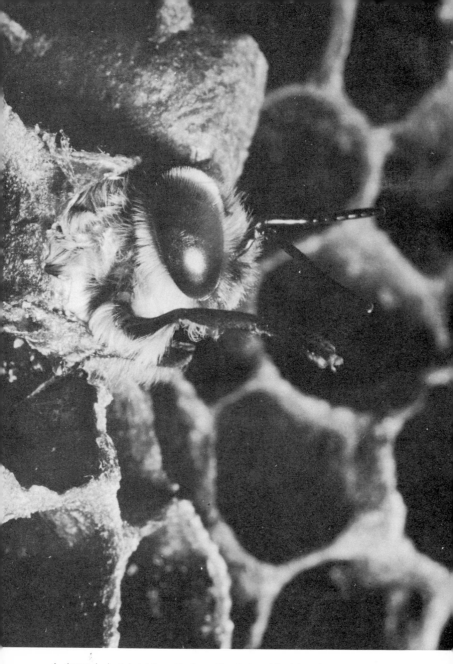

A drone is just hatching. He is easily distinguished by his huge eyes. Drones require 25 days to develop from egg to adult, longer than the worker eggs (21 days) or the queen (17).

# THE DRONES – PLAYBOYS OF THE BEE WORLD

ONLY ONE member of the honeybee family—the drone— escapes the duties of a society dedicated above all to the service of its colony. Born early in summer, and living one season, the drone's only duty is to pursue the queen on her mating flights. If he is successful, he mates with her; but for this privilege he dies immediately afterwards. The remainder of the drones pursue a short "playboy" life of ease, fed and tended by the workers while food is plentiful, flying about leisurely in the sunshine, even visiting other bee hives unmolested by the guards who would attack foreign worker bees.

Drones develop from those eggs of the queen which are not fertilized. It is not known if the worker bees cause the queen to lay unfertilized eggs by building large-size drone cells, or if the queen herself decides to lay drone eggs at certain times. Since it is the unfertilized eggs that develop into drones, it might be said that male bees have no male parent—only a queen for a mother.

Larger than worker bees but smaller than a queen, drones have shaggy coats which give them a blunt appearance. Their huge eyes are distinctive. These are indispensible if they are to sight the swiftly flying queen in the air on her short mating flight. In contrast to the hum of the workers, they emit a deep, booming—in fact, a droning—sound.

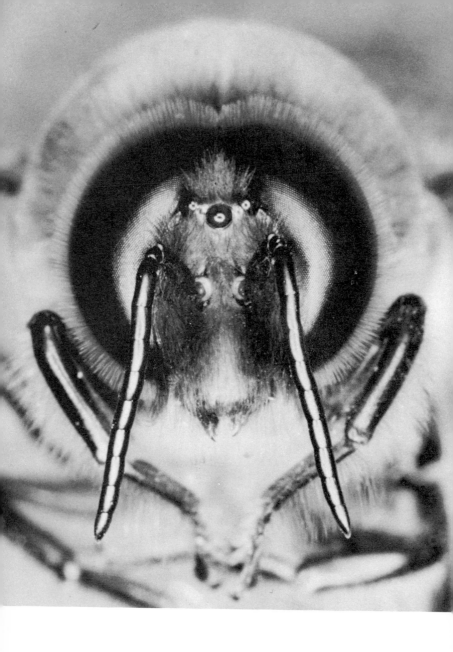

(Above) The enormous eyes of the drone take up most of his head. He needs good eyesight to find the queen in mid-air on the mating flight.

(Left, opposite page) With the vanity of a playboy, the drone poses for his picture. Notice the thick fur, as well as the large eyes. Drones are considerably larger than the female workers.

The lazy drones are not always tolerated in the hive and fed by the workers.

When they are no longer needed and food gets scarce, the worker bees pay no more attention to them. Disaster is brewing for the unsuspecting fellows. The previously friendly workers will try to make them leave the hive.

(Left, above) A battle between workers and drones has begun. The suddenly hostile workers hurry up from all sides and start to tug at an idler.

(Left, below) The battle is in full swing. More and more indignant workers hurry to the battlefield, trying to throw a drone off the landing board and prevent him from entering the flight hole.

(Above) Three bees at once try to prevent the drone from getting onto the landing board.

(Left) The battle ends. Most of the workers are already pursuing their normal occupations again. One last drone who does not want to accept his doom is yanked down from the landing board.

(Above) Unheeded, a few other defeated drones are left lying on the landing board after the end of the battle. They are no longer being fed, and since they cannot keep themselves alive, they will shortly be left to starve. Contrary to uninformed opinion, the workers seldom use their stingers during battles with the drones. They save up their valuable supply of venom for real enemies; the lazy playboys are not worth even a drop of poison to them any more.

# THE BEES' SENSE ORGANS

THE BEE's senses of smell (seated in its antennae) and of taste are roughly similar to a human being's, but its sight is completely different. In each of its two eyes, a queen has from 3,000 to 4,000 facets, a worker from 4,000 to 5,000 and a drone from 7,000 to 8,000 facets; but the bee can see only the rough outlines of its environment. It perceives only part of the range of coloration we know. Bees cannot see red, as we can. But they can see ultra-violet, which we cannot. Bees can do something else we cannot do: they are able to recognize polarized light. Because of this and because the light from different parts of the sky is differently polarized, depending on the sun's position, bees can orient themselves to the environment and find their way to and from the hive even when the sun is covered with clouds.

In addition to these complex eyes, the bees also have three simple eyes (*ocelli*) as were shown on the drone. We know very little about the functions of these simple eyes.

Whether a bee has a sense of hearing has not yet been determined, but its highly developed sense of touch may serve instead. This sense enables the bee to perceive the slightest vibration, possibly including some sound waves.

The bee's ability to feel temperature differences to within $\frac{1}{2}$ degree Fahrenheit is one of nature's marvels. Another is the bee's exceptional sense of balance. The fine hairs on its body may help maintain this equilibrium, along with the hairs only visible by microscope on the glittering upper surfaces of its wings. Experiments have shown that if these hairs are shaved off, the bee's equilibrium is seriously impaired.

A bee's eye facets enlarged 70 times. (A 6-foot man enlarged to this proportion would be 420 feet tall.)

An additional sense—the bee's sense of time—compares with a craftsman's precision-made watch in clocking the passage of hours. Bees were taken into a mine, and it was found that, even without the aid of sunlight, they knew when the food was served!

# THE LANGUAGE OF THE BEES

BEES ALWAYS live for the community. By means of their dance language they can communicate information about forage to each other. Scout bees returning from a source of nectar can convey the exact location of their discovery to workers waiting in the hive through special dance routines. By their scent they even disclose information about the kind of flower yielding the nectar.

By dancing round and round in a circle on the comb in the "round dance," the returning gatherer proclaims to the other bees: "Our discovery is in the immediate vicinity of the hive." Directions to more distant finds are given by the "sickle dance" and the "figure-of-eight" dance, in which the gatherers waggle or shift their tails while running along the comb. A tail waggled on a downward run means the direction is away from the sun; upward waggling tells that it is towards the sun; waggling at an angle indicates the corresponding angle of deviation from the sun. The frequency and duration of the waggling describes to within a few yards the distance to the crop: the faster the waggling, the closer the crop. Dances range in number from 5 to 50 per minute. In this dance language, the bee can estimate distances of 300 yards up to 6 miles and more for its fellow workers.

(Above) In the "round dance" on the comb, a returning scout tells the workers in the hive that the blossom is near the hive. (Below) The "figure-of-eight" dance. Running directly upwards while performing the "wag-tail" dance, this scout shows that the food is exactly in the direction of the sun.

# SWARMING

NATURE'S PLAN for all her creatures is always the same: to preserve and reproduce the species. Plants reproduce from seeds or shoots that continue to propagate more seeds; birds hatch their eggs and the young birds seek out new nesting grounds for themselves. But young bees cannot go off and start a new life of their own. As we have seen, all the bees in a colony, of all ages, are dependent upon each other. Therefore, the only way to reproduce is to start with a new colony and that is exactly what the bees do when they "swarm."

Swarming starts when a colony becomes so large that there is not enough queen substance to satisfy all the

Bee sucking up honey preparatory to emigrating in search of a new home.

This is the way a colony of bees without protection from the weather set up house outdoors. The bees protect the brood maturing within the cells of the comb from the cold night with a warming blanket of their bodies. A swarm in the open air can survive even long periods of bad weather during the summer months. The small colony of bees illustrated here could survive effortlessly from spring until late summer. In the end, however, such a swarm will inevitably be killed by the frost of a cold autumn and freezing winter. In the tropics, there are species of bees which build combs and live out-of-doors all the time.

workers. When that happens, the workers start building queen cells. They feed the larvae in these cells on royal jelly all the time and they respond to this rich food by developing all the attributes of a queen.

Since there can be only one queen in a colony, the old one must leave. For a long time the old queen has been so well-nourished that she is too heavy and too clumsy for flying. About a week before the hatching of the new queen, the old one is put on half rations to get her in condition for flying. On a thundery day shortly before the birth of the new monarch, the old queen leaves the hive. With her go at least half of the workers and drones. Before emigrating, or swarming, these bees suck themselves full of honey, for they will have to live without shelter and supplies of honey until they find a new home. What force or being decides which bees will swarm is still an unsolved mystery.

Emerging from the hive, the swarming bees shoot up into the air like a jet of water from a garden hose, seemingly swirling aimlessly back and forth but actually moving towards a branch or some other suitable temporary clustering site. By means of hooks on their feet the swarming bees cling to each other and form a tight cluster on the spot. A few bees, however, continue to fly around. These are the scout bees who serve as quartermasters on the lookout for a permanent home site, such as a hollow in a tree or a cave.

After finding a place that appeals to it, each scout returns to the swarm, and by means of its dance language tries to induce the swarm to move to the spot it has chosen, rather than to the other scouts' choices. The bees "vote" by clustering around the scout whose campaign appeals most to them. It seems as though one scout converts the other scouts too and all the dances

This swarm
settled on
my camera!

This swarm landed on my garden swing, probably because the old queen found flight too difficult and had to land on the first available spot. A few scouts have flown off in search of a permanent home. Since these bees filled themselves with honey before emigrating, they can hardly arch themselves to sting, and my little boy eating his breakfast right under them is safe from their barbs.

indicate the same new home. Then, and only then, the whole swarm flies off and follows this scout to its new dwelling.

Many misfortunes, however, can befall the swarming bees before they are safely settled in their new home. Bad weather can ground them. The quartermasters may not be able to find any suitable site, or perhaps the swarm cannot agree on a new site.

(Right) A veteran beekeeper rescued my camera from the swarm. First he set up a hive next to a table to entice the bees. Then he lifted the camera, and shook the bees off, onto the table.

(Below) The excited swarm investigates the man-made hive, finds it acceptable, and enters its new home through the flight hole.

# BEES IN THE SERVICE OF MANKIND

FOR MANY thousands of years men have studied these magicians of the insect world and have profited by their industry. As long ago as 389-295 B.C. the Greeks attached so much significance to the honeybee that they engraved its form on their coins. The Old Testament refers to bees many times—the haven of the ancient Israelites was the Promised Land of "milk and honey." Other ancient evidence of the honeybee's importance to mankind include a painting of honey being collected from a bee's nest, at least 7,000 years old in a cave in Spain. Also, numerous murals in ancient Egyptian graves depict honeybees.

Their wax brought the first artificial light of candles into man's shelter and provided the first modelling and sealing agents—for king's royal seals as well as house-

In America and England today, bees are kept in wooden hives which hold larger colonies than the straw skeps at the left. There are up to 50 hives in the same apiary. In some European countries, the hives are put side by side in a bee house. The picture above shows what great activity is concentrated in front of the hive entrance.

wives' preserves. For these reasons the craft of keeping bees was developed.

In very early times bees were kept in hollowed-out tree trunks and in coiled straw hives. Through the ages, beekeeping has grown into a very specialized science with great economic importance.

Books have been written about bees for more than 2,000 years, but this volume is one of the first to unfold the panorama of the birth of the bee in actual close-up photographs. It is my hope that it has opened your eyes to nature's miniature marvels in the wonderful and often mysterious world of the bees.